SANJEEV KAPOOR

Chatpati Chaat Recipes

In association with Alyona Kapoor

Popular Prakashan

www.popularprakashan.com

Published by
POPULAR PRAKASHAN PVT. LTD.
301, Mahalaxmi Chambers
22, Bhulabhai Desai Road
Mumbai - 400 026
for Khana Khazana Publications Pvt. Ltd.

First Published 2016

(4434)
ISBN: 978-81-7991-875-3

Design: Anjali Sawant
Photography: Bharat Bhirangi

PRINTED IN INDIA
by Saurabh Printers (P) Ltd.
Plot No. 67 A-68, Ecotech, Ext. I
Kasna, Greater Noida-201306 (U.P)

Author's Note

Chaat! Just the mention of this word sets everyone's taste buds watering including mine!

Chaat is very close to what Indian food generally is – chatpata! It is a scrumptious blend of teekha, meetha, khatta, namkeen – absolutely tasty. The word 'chaat' is derived from the Hindi verb 'chaatna' which literally means 'to lick one's fingers clean'.

Served cold and sometimes even hot it is a versatile any-time snack. And now varieties of chaat are found in plentiful across the length and breadth of India. Wherever you go you get chaat with, naturally, the local touch.

Savour a cocktail of seasonal fruits in Fruit Chaat or enjoy a wholesome Baby Uttappa with Aloo Bhaji, or better still gorge on a Chinese Bhel…unusual but tasty, they are all winners all the way!

Happy cooking!

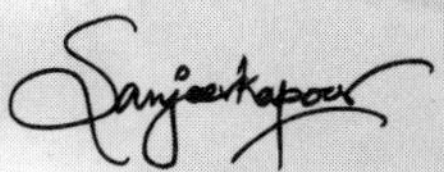

Contents

DILLI ALOO TIKKI CHAAT

Pattice

4 large potatoes

Salt to taste

Oil for shallow-frying

Filling

1 cup split black gram, soaked and boiled

1 tablespoon chopped fresh coriander leaves

2 green chillies, chopped

Black salt to taste

A pinch of asafoetida

½ inch ginger, chopped

½ teaspoon chaat masala

½ teaspoon red chilli powder

Topping (one portion)

½ cup matara (dried yellow peas), boiled

¼ cup yogurt

2 tablespoons Date and Tamarind Chutney (page 94)

½ tablespoon Green Coriander Chutney (page 95)

¼ teaspoon roasted cumin powder

¼ teaspoon chaat masala

¼ teaspoon red chilli powder

A few crisp, flat puris (papdi), crushed

- Boil, peel and grate the potatoes. Put them into a bowl, add salt and mix.
- In a separate bowl, combine the boiled dhuli urad dal, coriander leaves, green chillies, black salt, asafoetida, ginger, chaat masala and chilli powder.
- Knead the grated potatoes. Grease the palms of your hands. Place a portion of mashed potato on one palm, flatten slightly, make a hollow in the centre and stuff with the filling. Enclose the filling with the potato and shape into a thick round tikki.
- Heat sufficient oil on a non-stick tawa; add the tikki and shallow-fry till golden brown on both sides.
- To serve, place each pattice on a plate. Flatten the centre slightly and place a few matara in the hollow. Top with dollops of yogurt, date and tamarind chutney and green coriander chutney.
- Sprinkle with cumin powder, chaat masala and chilli powder. Crush a few flat puries and sprinkle over the chaat. Serve immediately.

ALOO ANAARDANA CHAAT

2 large potatoes, boiled and cut into 1-inch pieces

1 cup fresh pomegranate kernels

1 large onion, chopped

2 green chillies, chopped

½ cup roasted peanuts

2 tablespoons chopped fresh coriander leaves

1 tablespoon chopped fresh mint leaves

2 teaspoons chaat masala

Salt to taste

½ cup sev

1 teaspoon lemon juice

2 tablespoons Green Coriander Chutney (page 95)

- In a large bowl, combine the potatoes, pomegranate, onion, green chillies, peanuts, coriander leaves, mint leaves, chaat masala and salt and toss well to mix.
- Add the sev, lemon juice and green coriander chutney and toss again. Transfer the mixture to individual bowls and serve immediately.

BHAKARWADI CHAAT

1 cup mini bhakarwadi

½ cup bean sprouts

1 cup yogurt

Salt to taste

2 medium potatoes, boiled and finely chopped

1 large onion, finely chopped

5 tablespoons Green Coriander Chutney (page 95)

3 tablespoons Date and Tamarind Chutney (page 94)

1 teaspoon chaat masala

¼ teaspoon red chilli powder

1 teaspoon roasted cumin powder

¼ cup nylon sev

2 tablespoons chopped fresh coriander leaves

- Cook the bean sprouts in one and a half cups of boiling salted water for two or three minutes. Drain, refresh in cold water and set aside.

- Whisk yogurt with salt and place in a refrigerator to chill for half an hour.
- To prepare the chaat, arrange the bhakarwadi in a large serving plate; top with layers of moong sprouts, potatoes, onion and chilled yogurt.
- Drizzle both the chutneys and sprinkle chaat masala, chilli powder, cumin powder and nylon sev over the yogurt.
- Garnish with coriander leaves and serve immediately.

GREEN CHANA CHAAT

1½ cups dried green Bengal gram, soaked overnight

2 medium onions, chopped

2 medium tomatoes, chopped

2–3 green chillies, chopped

2 tablespoons chopped fresh coriander leaves

Black salt to taste

1 teaspoon roasted cumin powder

1 teaspoon chaat masala

½ teaspoon red chilli powder

2 tablespoons lemon juice

- Pressure-cook the soaked gram in three cups of water till the pressure is released two or three times (two or three whistles), or till tender.
- Transfer the chana to a non-stick kadai and simmer till all the water evaporates. Place the hot chana in a bowl.
- Add the onions, tomatoes, green chillies, coriander leaves, black salt, roasted cumin powder, chaat masala, chilli powder and lemon juice and mix well. Serve immediately.

KOTHIMBIR WADI CHAAT

1 cup chopped fresh coriander leaves

1 cup gram flour

4 green chillies, chopped

2 teaspoons grated jaggery

Salt to taste

A pinch of soda bicarbonate

½ teaspoon turmeric powder

2 tablespoons oil + for deep-frying

To serve

1½ cups farsan

1½ cups yogurt, whisked

4 tablespoons Green Coriander Chutney (page 95)

1 teaspoon chaat masala

2 tablespoons chopped fresh coriander leaves

- Combine one cup of coriander leaves, the gram flour, green chillies, jaggery, salt, soda bicarbonate, turmeric powder and two tablespoons of oil in a deep bowl.

- Add enough water to make a thick batter.
- Pour the batter into a greased tray. Place the tray in a pressure cooker or a steamer and steam over high heat for fifteen to twenty minutes or till firm and cooked. Remove, cool and cut into one-inch cubes.
- Heat plenty of oil in a kadai and deep-fry the kothimbir wadi till light golden brown and crisp. Drain on absorbent paper.
- To serve, divide the wadi between four individual bowls, top with farsan, drizzle some yogurt and green coriander chutney over and sprinkle with chaat masala and coriander leaves. Serve immediately.

PEANUT CHAAT

2 cups raw peanuts

1 tablespoon sea salt

1 teaspoon turmeric powder

Salt to taste

¼ teaspoon chaat masala

½ teaspoon red chilli powder

1 teaspoon roasted cumin powder

1 medium onion, chopped

1 medium tomato, chopped

2 green chillies, chopped

2 tablespoons chopped fresh coriander leaves

2 tablespoons lemon juice

- Pressure-cook the peanuts in five cups of water with sea salt and turmeric powder till the pressure is released four or five times (four or five whistles). Drain and shell the peanuts.
- Place the peanuts in a bowl. Add the salt, chaat masala, chilli powder, roasted cumin powder, onion, tomato, green chillies, coriander leaves, and lemon juice and mix well. Serve hot or cold.

KACHORI CHAAT

1 cup refined flour

¼ teaspoon carom seeds

¼ teaspoon salt

A pinch of soda bicarbonate

2 tablespoons pure ghee

Filling

½ cup shelled green peas, lightly crushed

½ tablespoon oil + for deep-frying

A pinch of asafoetida

¼ teaspoon cumin seeds

½ inch ginger, chopped

2 green chillies, chopped

Salt to taste

¼ teaspoon garam masala powder

2 tablespoons grated coconut

2 tablespoons roasted peanuts, crushed

Topping

2 cups yogurt, whisked and chilled

1 teaspoon red chilli powder

2 teaspoons roasted cumin powder

4 teaspoons Green Coriander Chutney (page 95)

4 teaspoons Date and Tamarind Chutney (page 94)

- For the filling, heat the oil in a non-stick pan; add the asafoetida and cumin seeds. When the cumin seeds begin to change colour, add the ginger, green chillies, green peas and salt.
- Mix and cook for two or three minutes. Remove from heat and stir in the garam masala powder. Set aside to cool. When completely cold, add the coconut and peanuts and mix well. Divide the filling into eight equal portions. Set aside.
- For the kachoris, mix together the refined flour, carom seeds, salt, soda bicarbonate and pure ghee in a bowl. Add enough cold water and knead into a stiff dough.
- Divide the dough into eight equal portions. Roll out each portion and press to make round puris. Stuff each puri with the stuffing and shape into a kachori.
- Heat plenty of oil in a kadai and deep-fry the kachoris in moderately hot oil till crisp and golden. Drain on absorbent paper.
- To serve, lightly crush two to three kachoris and place them in individual serving bowls.
- Pour some yogurt over, sprinkle chilli powder and cumin powder, drizzle both the chutneys and serve immediately.

TAWA PANEER CHAAT

500 grams cottage cheese, cut into ½-inch pieces

Crisp puffed puris (as for paani puri)

3 tablespoons oil

2 large onions, chopped

1 teaspoon ginger paste

1 teaspoon garlic paste

3–4 green chillies, seeded and chopped

¾ cup tomato purée

3–4 tablespoons pav bhaji masala

Salt to taste

½ tablespoon chaat masala

2-3 tablespoons chopped fresh coriander leaves

- Heat the oil on a non-stick tawa; add the onions and sauté till brown. Add the ginger paste and garlic paste and continue to sauté for a few minutes.
- Add a little water and continue to sauté for one minute. Add the green chillies and sauté for another minute.

- Add the tomato purée, pav bhaji masala, salt and chaat masala and continue to cook over a low heat till the oil separates from the masala.
- Add the cubed cottage cheese and half the coriander leaves and stir gently to mix. Check seasoning and cook over a low heat for two minutes.
- Make small holes in each puri and stuff with the cottage cheese mixture. Serve, garnished with the remaining coriander leaves.

MAKAI KA CHIWDA CHAAT

2 cups makai ka chiwda

1 large potato, boiled, peeled and diced

1 medium onion, chopped

1 large cucumber, seeded and diced

1 large tomato, seeded and diced

2 tablespoons chopped unripe green mango

Salt to taste

1 green chilli, chopped

1 teaspoon chaat masala

2 teaspoons lemon juice

2 tablespoons chopped fresh coriander leaves

¼ cup sliced fresh coconut

- In a large bowl, combine the potato, onion, cucumber, tomato, green mango, salt, green chilli and chaat masala and toss to mix well.
- Add the makai ka chiwda, lemon juice and toss again to mix.
- Transfer to a serving bowl. Garnish with coriander leaves and coconut slices and serve immediately.

DILLI ALOO KACHALU CHAAT

2 large potatoes, cut into 1-inch pieces

1 large sweet potato, cut into 1-inch pieces

1 inch ginger, cut into thin strips

2 teaspoons lemon juice

Salt to taste

Oil for shallow-frying

1 tablespoon Date and Tamarind Chutney (page 94)

1 teaspoon chaat masala

½ teaspoon red chilli powder

2 teaspoons roasted cumin powder

2 green chillies, chopped

3 tablespoons chopped fresh coriander leaves

- Place the ginger in a small bowl; add one teaspoon of lemon juice and a pinch of salt, mix well and chill in a refrigerator till ready to use.
- Heat the oil on a thick non-stick tawa till moderately hot.

- Add the potatoes and shallow-fry till crisp and golden. Drain on absorbent paper.
- To the same oil, add the sweet potato and shallow-fry till crisp and golden. Drain on absorbent paper.
- Transfer the potatoes and sweet potatoes to a large bowl. Add the salt, date and tamarind chutney, chaat masala, chilli powder, cumin powder, green chillies, coriander leaves and the remaining lemon juice and mix well.
- To serve, transfer the mixture to a serving bowl, garnish with ginger strips.
- Serve immediately.

KARELA CHAAT

2 cups refined flour

Salt to taste

8–10 black peppercorns, crushed

4 tablespoons ghee, melted

2 cups yogurt, whisked

2 teaspoons sugar

Oil for deep-frying

1 cup Green Coriander Chutney (page 95)

Black salt to taste

2 medium boiled potatoes, cut into ½-inch pieces

1 cup Date and Tamarind Chutney (page 94)

1 teaspoon red chilli powder

1 teaspoon roasted cumin powder

1 cup sev

2 tablespoons chopped fresh coriander leaves

- Combine the flour, salt, crushed peppercorns and ghee in a bowl.
- Add some cold water and knead into a dough.

- Roll the dough out into thin sheets. Cover and set aside to rest for a while.
- Combine the yogurt and sugar in a bowl. Strain and squeeze through a piece of muslin into another bowl. Set aside.
- To make the karelas, cut the rolled out dough into six-inch by four-inch rectangles.
- Make small slits at even intervals and moisten the edges with water. Roll up the pieces and press the edges together to seal.
- Heat sufficient oil till moderately hot in a kadai. Deep-fry the karelas till golden. Drain on absorbent paper.
- Place a couple of karelas on a plate. Top with yogurt, green coriander chutney, black salt, potatoes, date and tamarind chutney, more yogurt, chilli powder, roasted cumin powder, sev and coriander leaves.
- Garnish with a whole fried or crushed karela. Serve immediately.

DHOKLA CHAAT

500 grams khaman dhokla, cut into 1½-inch cubes

1½ cups skimmed milk yogurt, whisked

3 tablespoons Green Coriander Chutney (page 95)

3 tablespoons Date and Tamarind Chutney (page 94)

Sev, as required

4 tablespoons chopped fresh coriander leaves

- Place the dhokla in a large serving dish. Pour the yogurt over and drizzle with both the chutneys.
- Sprinkle sev generously on top and serve immediately, garnished with coriander leaves.

MEXICAN CHAAT

25–30 tortilla or corn chips, crushed

1 cup corn kernels, boiled

2 medium potatoes, boiled and chopped

1 large onion, chopped

1 large tomato, chopped

1 jalapeño chilli, chopped

2–3 tablespoons Green Coriander Chutney (page 95)

3–4 tablespoons Date and Tamarind Chutney (page 94)

Salt to taste

1 cup yogurt, whisked and chilled

1 tablespoon chopped fresh coriander leaves

- Chill the yogurt in a refrigerator.
- In a large bowl, combine the crushed corn chips, reserving some for garnishing, corn, potatoes, onion, tomato, jalapeño chilli, two tablespoons of green coriander chutney, three tablespoons of date and tamarind chutney and salt; toss well to mix.

- Add the chilled yogurt and mix well with a spoon or a spatula.
- Transfer the mixture to a platter, drizzle the remaining green coriander chutney and date and tamarind chutney on top.
- Serve, garnished with the reserved corn chips and the coriander leaves.

FARALI CHAAT

500 grams purple yam, boiled and cut into small cubes

2–3 tablespoons pure ghee

1 teaspoon cumin seeds

3 green chillies, chopped

2 teaspoons red chilli powder

3 tablespoons chopped fresh coriander leaves

Rock salt to taste

1½ cups yogurt, whisked and chilled

4 teaspoons Green Coriander Chutney (page 95)

4 teaspoons Date and Tamarind Chutney (page 94)

1 cup farali chiwda

- Heat the ghee in a kadai; add the cumin seeds and sauté over a medium heat till they change colour.
- Add the green chillies and sauté for half a minute. Add the yam, chilli powder, coriander leaves and rock salt and sauté for one minute, stirring and tossing continuously.
- Transfer the mixture to four serving plates. Pour three or four tablespoons of chilled yogurt over each portion.
- Drizzle one teaspoon each of green coriander chutney and date and tamarind chutney, sprinkle one-fourth cup of farali chiwda and serve immediately.

KATORI CHAAT

5 medium potatoes

2 tablespoons oil + for deep-frying

Chole filling (page 74), as required

4 tablespoons thick yogurt

Date and Tamarind Chutney (page 94), as required

Green Coriander Chutney (page 95), as required

Sev, as required

2–3 tablespoons chopped fresh coriander leaves

- Grate the potatoes and soak them in water for five minutes. Drain thoroughly and spread on absorbent kitchen paper to dry. Divide into four portions.
- Take two small strainers – one slightly larger than the other.
- Heat plenty of oil in a kadai. For each katori, layer the bigger strainer with one portion of the grated potatoes. Place the other strainer over the potato layer and press lightly.

- Gently lower both the strainers together into the hot oil and deep-fry till golden. Drain on absorbent paper and set aside.
- Fill the chole in each of the fried katoris. Drizzle one tablespoon of yogurt over each.
- Top with date and tamarind chutney and green coriander chutney. Sprinkle sev and coriander leaves and serve immediately.

PAPDI CHAAT

20 crisp flat puris (papdi)

2 medium potatoes, boiled and sliced

1 large onion, sliced

2–3 tablespoons Date and Tamarind Chutney (page 94)

2 tablespoons Green Coriander Chutney (page 95)

1 teaspoon lemon juice

1 teaspoon roasted cumin powder

1 teaspoon chaat masala

½ teaspoon rock salt

¼ cup yogurt, whisked and chilled

1 cup sev

2 tablespoons fresh pomegranate kernels

2 tablespoons chopped fresh coriander leaves

- Arrange the papdi on a serving dish. Place a potato slice on each papdi and then top with a slice of onion. Drizzle date and tamarind chutney and green coriander chutney on each papdi.
- Sprinkle the lemon juice, cumin powder, chaat masala and rock salt over the papdi and drizzle some yogurt over.
- Top with the sev, pomegranate kernels and coriander leaves and serve immediately.

MASALA DOSA CHAAT

2 cups dosa batter

Red Chilli-Garlic Chutney (page 96), as required

1½ cups potato bhaji, lightly mashed

2 large onions, chopped

2 large tomatoes, chopped

1 teaspoon red chilli powder

1½ teaspoons chaat masala

Oil for shallow-frying

2 tablespoons chopped fresh coriander leaves

Ragda

½ cup dried white peas, soaked overnight

¼ teaspoon turmeric powder

A pinch of asafoetida

Salt to taste

2 teaspoons chaat masala

2 teaspoons Date and Tamarind Chutney (page 94)

- For the ragda, pressure-cook white peas in three cups of water with turmeric powder, asafoetida and salt till the pressure is released four or five times (four or five whistles), or till soft. Mash the peas slightly. Add the chaat masala and date and tamarind chutney and a little water if too thick and simmer for ten minutes. Keep the ragda hot.

- Heat and season a dosa non-stick tawa. Place a small ladleful of dosa batter on the tawa and spread evenly to make an eight-inch diameter dosa. Drizzle half a teaspoon of oil round the dosa and cook over a low heat for half a minute.

- Spread a little chilli-garlic chutney all over the dosa. Sprinkle with some onions, tomatoes, chilli powder and chaat masala. Place a small portion of potato bhaji in the centre.

- Press gently with the back of a ladle till lightly mashed and spread all over the dosa. Drizzle some more oil and cook over a low heat so that the underside turns golden and crisp.

- Roll the dosa up tightly like a spring roll, transfer onto a plate and cut into equal lengths and arrange on a serving platter.

- Spoon ragda generously over the dosa, garnish with coriander leaves and serve hot.

FRUIT CHAAT

½ small papaya, cut into 1-inch cubes

2 kiwi fruits, cut into 1-inch cubes

½ cup fresh pomegranate kernels

½ cup orange segments

½ cup sweet lime segments

1 medium apple, cut into 1-inch cubes

¼ cup seedless green grapes, halved

¼ cup seedless black grapes, halved

½ teaspoon red chilli powder

1½ tablespoons chaat masala

Rock salt to taste

1 tablespoon lemon juice

- Combine the papaya, kiwi fruit, pomegranate kernels, orange and sweet lime segments, apple and green and black grapes in a large bowl and place in a refrigerator to chill thoroughly.
- Just before serving, sprinkle with chilli powder, chaat masala and rock salt. Add the lemon juice and toss gently to mix. Serve immediately.

MASALA SANDWICH DOUBLE ROTI CHAAT

8 pav

4 medium potatoes, boiled and mashed

2 teaspoons oil

½ teaspoon mustard seeds

1 teaspoon red chilli powder

¼ teaspoon turmeric powder

½ teaspoon garam masala powder

Salt to taste

3–4 tablespoons butter

4 tablespoons Green Coriander Chutney (page 95)

4 tablespoons Date and Tamarind Chutney (page 94)

1 medium onion, chopped

8 tablespoons sev

4 tablespoons chopped fresh coriander leaves

- Heat the oil in a non-stick pan; add the mustard seeds. When they begin to splutter, add the mashed potatoes, chilli powder, turmeric powder, garam masala powder and salt.

- Mix well and cook for three or four minutes. Remove and set aside.
- Slit two pav horizontally, but do not cut through to separate the halves.
- Spread some butter on the insides of the pav. Stuff with the potato mixture and lightly toast the pav on a non-stick tawa using a little butter.
- Arrange two roasted pav on each serving plate. Top with green coriander chutney, date and tamarind chutney, onion and a generous helping of sev.
- Garnish with coriander leaves and serve immediately.

KHASTA ALOO CHAAT

4 large potatoes, boiled and mashed

Salt to taste

2 tablespoons cornflour

Oil for deep-frying

½ cup thick Green Coriander Chutney (page 95)

4–5 tablespoons arrowroot flour

1 tablespoon Red Chilli-Garlic Chutney (page 96)

4–5 tablespoons Date and Tamarind Chutney (page 94)

1 teaspoon chaat masala

- In a large bowl, combine the potatoes with salt and cornflour and mix well. Divide the potato mixture into sixteen equal portions and shape into lemon-sized balls.
- Flatten a portion of mashed potato on your palm and place one teaspoon of green coriander chutney in the centre.

- Bring the sides together to enclose the filling and shape into small squares. Dust with a little arrowroot flour and set aside.
- Heat sufficient oil in a kadai and deep-fry the squares, a few at a time, till golden brown. Drain on absorbent paper.
- Place the fried potato squares on individual serving plates, drizzle with red chilli-garlic chutney and date and tamarind chutney, sprinkle chaat masala and serve immediately.

PALAK PAKORE KI CHAAT

16–20 fresh medium-sized spinach leaves

1½ cups coarse gram flour

Salt to taste

½ teaspoon red chilli powder

¼ teaspoon turmeric powder

½ teaspoon carom seeds

A pinch of asafoetida

Oil for deep-frying

1 cup yogurt

2 teaspoons roasted cumin powder

4 tablespoons Green Coriander Chutney (page 95)

4 tablespoons Date and Tamarind Chutney (page 94)

3 medium onions, chopped

½ cup sev

½ cup chopped fresh coriander leaves

- In a bowl, combine the gram flour, salt, chilli powder, turmeric powder, carom seeds and asafoetida. Add sufficient water to make a thin batter.

- Heat sufficient oil in a kadai. Coat each spinach leaf with batter on both sides and deep-fry till golden brown and crisp. Drain on absorbent paper.
- Whisk yogurt with salt to taste.
- For each serving, place two pakore on a plate. Cover with two or three tablespoons of whisked yogurt and sprinkle with cumin powder.
- Top with dollops of green coriander chutney and date and tamarind chutney.
- Sprinkle some chopped onions and cover liberally with sev. Garnish with coriander leaves and serve immediately.

HEALTHY CORNFLAKES BHEL

2 cups cornflakes

1 large potato, boiled and diced

1 medium onion, chopped

1 large cucumber, seeded and diced

1 large tomato, seeded and diced

1 cup fresh pomegranate kernels

Salt to taste

1 teaspoon chaat masala

2 tablespoons unripe green mango, chopped

2 tablespoons chopped fresh coriander leaves

2 teaspoons lemon juice

- In a large bowl, combine the potato, onion, cucumber, tomato, pomegranate, salt, chaat masala and green mango and toss well to mix.
- Add the cornflakes, coriander leaves and lemon juice and toss again to mix well. Transfer the bhel to a serving bowl and serve immediately.

RAGDA PATTICE

1¼ cups dried white peas

4 large potatoes, boiled, peeled and mashed

¼ teaspoon turmeric powder

A pinch asafoetida

Salt to taste

2 tablespoons cornflour

2–3 green chillies, chopped

Oil for shallow-frying

Green Coriander Chutney (page 95), as required

Date and Tamarind Chutney (page 94), as required

2 medium onions, chopped

2 teaspoons chaat masala

2 tablespoons chopped fresh coriander leaves

- Soak the dried peas in three cups of water for about six hours.
- Drain and boil in three or four cups of water with turmeric powder, asafoetida and salt till soft. Mash the peas slightly.

- Add a little water if too thick and simmer for ten minutes. Keep the ragda hot.
- Add the cornflour, green chillies and salt to the mashed potato and mix well. Divide into eight equal portions, shape into balls and flatten slightly into pattice.
- Heat a little oil in a non-stick frying pan and fry the pattice gently on both sides over a medium heat till evenly browned. Keep warm.
- To serve, place two pattice on a plate and spoon some ragda over.
- Drizzle green coriander chutney and date and tamarind chutney over the top and sprinkle with onion, chaat masala and coriander leaves. Serve immediately.

SAMOSA CHOLE

4 samosas

Chole Filling (page 74), as required

4 tablespoons yogurt, whisked

4 tablespoons Date and Tamarind Chutney (page 94)

4 tablespoons Green Coriander Chutney (page 95)

- To serve, place the samosas on a serving platter, crush lightly and top with a generous portion of the chole.
- Pour yogurt over the chole, drizzle date and tamarind chutney and green coriander chutney and serve hot.

MASALA KHICHIA PAPAD

8 khichia papad

8 teaspoons butter

4 tablespoons Green Coriander Chutney (page 95)

2 tablespoons Red Chilli-Garlic Chutney (page 96)

2 tablespoons chaat masala

4–5 tablespoons chopped fresh coriander leaves

- Dry-roast all the khichia papad till crisp.
- Drizzle one teaspoon of butter over each papad and top with dollops of the chutneys.
- Sprinkle chaat masala and coriander leaves and serve immediately before the papad becomes soggy.

INSTANT DAHI WADE

8 large jeera butter biscuits

4 cups thin buttermilk

2½ cups yogurt, whisked and chilled

½ teaspoon rock salt

1 teaspoon red chilli powder

1 teaspoon roasted cumin powder

½ cup Date and Tamarind Chutney (page 94)

¼ cup chopped fresh coriander leaves

- Soak the jeera biscuits in buttermilk for eight to ten minutes till soft. Drain, squeeze lightly between your palms and set aside.
- Alternatively, soak the biscuits in four cups of warm water for four or five minutes and drain. Place two soaked biscuits in each serving bowl, and pour chilled yogurt over the biscuits.
- Serve, garnished with rock salt, chilli powder, cumin powder, date and tamarind chutney and coriander leaves.

PAPDI PIZZA

20 flat crisp puris

1 large onion

¼ cup pizza sauce

2 medium potatoes, boiled and sliced

¾ cup grated mozzarella cheese

2 medium green capsicums, sliced horizontally

Nylon sev, as required

- Preheat the oven to 180°C/350°F/Gas Mark 4.
- Cut the onion into thick round slices and separate the rings. Grease a baking tray and arrange the papdis on it. Spread the pizza sauce on the papdis. Place potato slices on some papdi and onion rings on the rest.
- Place the grated cheese in small heaps on each papdi and place green capsicum slices on some of them.
- Sprinkle with nylon sev. Put a little pizza sauce on top of some of the papdi pizzas. Bake in the preheated oven till the cheese melts. Serve hot.

DAHI BHALLE

¾ cup skinless split black gram

Salt to taste

15–20 raisins

1 inch ginger, chopped

2 green chillies, chopped

2 tablespoons gram flour

Oil for deep-frying

4–5 cups yogurt

1 teaspoon rock salt

1 tablespoon sugar

Green Coriander Chutney (page 95), as required

Date and Tamarind Chutney (page 94), as required

2 teaspoons roasted cumin powder

2 tablespoons chopped fresh coriander leaves

- Wash and soak the black gram in three cups of cold water overnight. Drain excess water the following day and grind the black gram to a smooth paste.

- Add the salt, raisins, ginger, green chillies and gram flour to the batter and whisk for ten minutes to make a fluffy batter.
- Heat sufficient oil in a kadai. Drop the batter in tablespoonfuls into the hot oil and fry the bhalle until light golden.
- Drain the bhalle on absorbent paper and soak in plenty of water for two minutes. Squeeze between your palms to drain out water.
- Whisk the yogurt well with rock salt and sugar to taste.
- To serve, place bhalle on a plate and cover with yogurt. Drizzle green coriander chutney and date and tamarind chutney on top and sprinkle with roasted cumin powder.
- Garnish with coriander leaves and serve immediately.

Chef's Tip

You can stuff the bhalle with a mixture of raisins, crushed cashew nuts and chopped coriander leaves to make Kalmi Wade. In which case, do not add raisins to the black gram batter.

FRIED GARADU INDORI STYLE

700–800 grams garadu (see note)

Oil for deep-frying

2 tablespoons Jiralu Masala (page 62)

Salt to taste

2 tablespoons lemon juice

2 tablespoons chopped fresh coriander leaves

- Trim the narrow tapering ends of the garadu and use only the middle section. Grease a knife and remove the peel. Cut garadu into large chunks.
- Boil seven to eight cups of water in a deep non-stick pan. Add garadu chunks and boil till just done.
- To check, insert a knife into the thickest part of the garadu after six to seven minutes.
- If it goes in easily the garadu is cooked. Remove from heat and place in a colander to drain. Leave to cool completely.

- Chop the garadu into small bite-sized squares.
- Heat sufficient oil in a kadai over a high heat. Deep-fry the garadu till lightly coloured. Drain on absorbent paper.
- Just before serving, refry the garadu in moderately hot oil till crisp. Drain on absorbent paper.
- Divide the fried garadu equally between serving plates, sprinkle jiralu masala powder, salt, lemon juice and coriander leaves and serve immediately.

Note:

- Garadu is a type of yam. It is somewhat like sweet potato in appearance.
- To make Jiralu Masala, mix together 2 teaspoons roasted cumin powder, 1½ teaspoons dried ginger powder, ½ teaspoon red chilli powder, ¼ teaspoon turmeric powder, a pinch of asafoetida, ½ teaspoon black salt, ½ teaspoon rock salt.

CHATPATI SHANKERPALI

2 cups savoury shankerpali, crushed

1 large onion, chopped

1 large tomato, seeded and chopped

3 green chillies, chopped

1 small unripe green mango, chopped

¼ cup masala chana dal

½ cup tikha sev

3 tablespoons chopped fresh coriander leaves

4 teaspoons Green Coriander Chutney (page 95)

1½ tablespoons Date and Tamarind Chutney (page 94)

1 teaspoon lemon juice

Salt to taste

- In a large bowl, combine the crushed shankerpali, onion, tomato, green chillies, green mango, masala chana dal and tikha sev and toss to mix well.
- Add the coriander leaves, green coriander chutney, date and tamarind chutney, lemon juice and salt and toss again. Spoon into four individual bowls and serve immediately.

RAJ KACHORI WITH CHOLE

¼ cup semolina

2 tablespoons refined flour

¼ teaspoon red chilli powder

Salt to taste

Oil for deep-frying

Filling

2 tablespoons gram flour

A pinch of soda bicarbonate

¼ teaspoon red chilli powder

Salt to taste

¼ teaspoon fennel powder

A pinch of black pepper powder

1½ tablespoons oil

Topping

1 cup Chole Filling (page 74)

1 cup yogurt, whisked

½ cup Date and Tamarind Chutney (page 94)

2 tablespoons Green Coriander Chutney (page 95)

1 teaspoon roasted cumin powder

½ teaspoon rock salt

1 teaspoon red chilli powder

½ cup sev

2–3 tablespoons chopped fresh coriander leaves

- Make a stiff dough of semolina, refined flour, chilli powder, salt and water.
- For the filling, mix together gram flour, soda bicarbonate, chilli powder, salt, fennel powder, pepper powder and oil. Add sufficient water and knead into a dough.
- Divide both the semolina dough and the gram flour dough into four equal parts each.
- Spread each portion of the semolina dough on your palm and place one portion of the gram flour dough in the centre. Gather the edges and shape into a ball. Further roll into a kachori.
- Heat sufficient oil in a kadai and deep-fry the kachoris over medium heat, turning once, till puffed up and crisp. Drain on absorbent paper and leave to cool. If they soften when cool, deep-fry again.
- To serve, place each kachori on a serving plate. Make a large hole in the centre and fill with a generous portion of chole. Pour one-fourth cup of yogurt over, and top with dollops of both the chutneys.
- Sprinkle cumin powder, rock salt, chilli powder, sev and coriander leaves over everything. Serve immediately.

JHAAL MURI

2 cups puffed rice

1 medium onion, chopped

¼ cup sprouted whole black gram, boiled

1 small cucumber, cut into ½-inch cubes

1 small tomato, seeded and cut into ½-inch cubes

2 green chillies, chopped

2 tablespoons roasted peanuts, skinned

2 tablespoons chopped fresh coriander leaves

2 tablespoons mustard oil (taken from a pickle)

2 tablespoons Jhaal Muri Masala (page 67)

Fresh coconut, sliced, to garnish

- In a large bowl, combine the puffed rice, onion, sprouted black gram, cucumber, tomato, green chillies, peanuts, and coriander leaves and toss to mix well.
- Add the mustard oil and jhaal muri masala and toss again to mix. Serve immediately, garnished with sliced coconut.

Note:

- For the Jhaal Muri Masala, mix together 1 teaspoon rock salt, 1 tablespoon roasted cumin power, ½ tablespoon red chilli powder, 1 teaspoon chaat masala and ½ teaspoon white pepper powder.

- If you do not have a pickle containing mustard oil, heat 2 tablespoons of mustard oil in a non-stick pan to smoking point. Take it off the heat, add ½ teaspoon mustard seeds, ¼ teaspoon fenugreek seeds, ¼ teaspoon fennel seeds, ½ teaspoon red chilli powder and a pinch of asafoetida. Leave to stand for one hour, strain and use.

BHUNA BHUTTA

2 American corn cobs

Salt to taste

2 tablespoons butter

2 tablespoons lemon juice

1 teaspoon red chilli flakes

1 teaspoon red chilli powder

2 teaspoons brown sugar

- Remove the husks of the corn. Place each cob on a twelve-inch square piece of aluminium foil.
- Either sprinkle with salt and brush with butter and lemon juice, or sprinkle salt, chilli flakes, chilli powder and brown sugar, and brush with butter and lemon juice.
- Wrap the aluminium foil around the cobs and twist the ends as for a toffee. Place on live charcoals or on a grill and cook for fifteen minutes.
- Open the foil wrapping and serve hot.

BABY UTTAPPA WITH ALOO BHAJI

2 cups ready-mixed uttappam batter

Oil, as required

½ cup aloo bhaji

8 tablespoons grated mozzarella cheese

2 teaspoons Red Chilli-Garlic Chutney (page 96)

4 teaspoons Green Coriander Chutney (page 95)

4 teaspoons Date and Tamarind Chutney (page 94)

6 tablespoons sev

- Heat a non-stick tawa and grease it lightly.
- For each uttappa, pour one ladleful of batter onto the tawa and spread with the back of the ladle to make a moderately thick three-inch round uttappa.
- Drizzle some oil all around.

- Spread a little aloo bhaji on top and cook till the base is pale gold.
- Sprinkle mozzarella cheese over the bhaji, cover the pan and cook till the cheese melts.
- Turn out the uttappa onto a serving plate. Spread all the three chutneys over the top, sprinkle sev and serve immediately. Make the remaining uttappa in the same way.

SEV BATATA PURI

24 crisp flat puris

2 large potatoes, boiled, peeled and chopped

1 small green unripe mango, chopped

Salt to taste

¼ teaspoon red chilli powder

2 medium onions, chopped

¼ cup Green Coriander Chutney (page 95)

2 tablespoons Red Chilli-Garlic Chutney (page 96)

¼ cup Date and Tamarind Chutney (page 94)

1 cup sev

½ tablespoon chaat masala

2 tablespoons chopped coriander leaves

- Arrange the puris on a plate.
- Mix together the potatoes, green mango, salt and chilli powder.
- Place portions of the mixture on the puris. Sprinkle the onion over the potato mixture.
- Drizzle green coriander chutney, red chilli-garlic chutney and date and tamarind chutney over the top.
- Cover the puris with plenty of sev.
- Sprinkle chaat masala and coriander leaves and serve immediately.

CANAPÉS WITH CHOLE

16 canapé cases, fried

1½ cups yogurt, whisked and chilled

1 teaspoon red chilli powder

2 teaspoons roasted cumin powder

2 teaspoons chaat masala

¼ cup Green Coriander Chutney (page)

Chole

1 cup chickpeas, soaked

Salt to taste

2 teaspoons tea leaves

2 tablespoons ghee

2 medium onions, chopped

1 teaspoon ginger paste

1 teaspoon garlic paste

4 tablespoons chole masala

¾ cup fresh tomato purée

4 tablespoons chopped fresh coriander leaves

- To make the chole, place the chickpeas with three cups of water and salt in a pressure cooker. Tie up the tea leaves in a piece of muslin to make a potli; add to the chickpeas.

- Close the lid and cook till the pressure is released five to six times (five to six whistles) or till the chickpeas are soft. Discard the potli. Drain and set aside. Reserve one-fourth cup of stock for cooking.
- Heat two tablespoons of ghee in a non-stick kadai; add the onions and sauté over a low heat till light golden. Add the ginger paste and garlic paste and sauté for half a minute.
- Add three tablespoons of chole masala and continue to sauté for another minute. Add the tomato purée and cook over a low heat for two to three minutes.
- Add the boiled chickpeas and the reserved stock and simmer for five minutes, or till all the water is absorbed and the ghee rises to the surface.
- Sprinkle the remaining chole masala and coriander leaves, stir and cover immediately. Remove from heat and keep warm.
- Place canapés on individual serving plates. Fill each canapé with two to three tablespoons of prepared chole. Pour some whisked yogurt over and sprinkle a little chilli powder, roasted cumin powder and chaat masala.
- Finally drizzle a little green coriander chutney on each canapé and serve immediately.

CHINESE BHEL

- 200 grams eggless noodles
- Salt to taste
- 1 tablespoon oil + for deep-frying
- 2–3 spring onions, sliced
- ½ cup bean sprouts
- ¼ cup roasted peanuts, crushed
- 1 tablespoon Sichuan sauce
- 1 tablespoon tomato ketchup
- Sliced spring onion greens, for garnishing

- Cook the noodles in six to eight cups of boiling salted water, to which one tablespoon of oil has been added, till almost done.
- Drain, refresh in cold water, drain again and spread on a large plate to cool.
- Heat sufficient oil in a wok and deep-fry noodles till crisp and golden brown. Drain on absorbent paper and leave to cool. Lightly crush the fried noodles.

- In a large bowl, combine the crushed noodles, spring onions, bean sprouts and peanuts and toss to mix.
- Add the Sichuan sauce and tomato ketchup and toss the mixture once more. Adjust seasoning. Serve in individual plates, garnished with spring onion greens.

DABELI

4 pav

1½ tablespoons dabeli masala powder

3 tablespoons oil

2 large potatoes, boiled, peeled and mashed

Salt to taste

1 teaspoon lemon juice

1 cup Date and Tamarind Chutney (page 94)

1 tablespoon sugar

½ cup masala peanuts

¼ cup grated fresh coconut

¼ cup fresh pomegranate kernels

10–12 black grapes, chopped

1 cup nylon sev

2 tablespoons fresh coriander leaves, chopped

¼ cup Red Chilli-Garlic Chutney (page 96)

2 medium onions, finely chopped

2 tablespoons butter

- Heat sufficient oil in a non-stick pan; add the potato, salt and a little water. Mix well and add the dabeli masala, lemon juice, a quarter cup of date and tamarind chutney and sugar. Mix and cook till quite dry.
- Spread the mixture on a plate. Sprinkle masala peanuts, grated coconut, pomegranate, black grapes, half the sev and coriander leaves on top.
- Slit the pavs horizontally without cutting through. Spread the red chilli-garlic chutney, a layer each of the potato stuffing, tamarind chutney, onion and sev in between the two halves.
- Place the stuffed pav on a hot non-stick tawa. Press lightly, spread with a little butter and toast on both sides, till heated through and slightly crisp. Serve hot.

AMERICAN SEV PURI

1 cup American sweet corn, boiled

½ cup sev

24 canapé cases

1 tablespoon oil + for deep-frying

1 medium onion, chopped

2 fresh red chillies, chopped

¼ cup sweet chilli sauce

½ teaspoon chaat masala

1 tablespoon chopped fresh mint leaves

2 tablespoons chopped fresh coriander leaves

1 tablespoon lemon juice

2 tablespoons chopped fresh parsley

- Heat one tablespoon of oil in a non-stick pan; add the onion and sauté for a while.
- Add the corn and sauté for a few minutes. Add the red chillies and sweet chilli sauce and toss to mix.

- Add the chaat masala, mint leaves and coriander leaves. Mix and cook till dry.
- Heat sufficient oil in a kadai and deep-fry the canapés lightly, taking care that they do not burn.
- Drain well on absorbent paper. Set aside to cool.
- Add the lemon juice to the corn mixture and mix well. Spoon into the canapés and sprinkle with sev.
- Garnish with parsley and serve immediately.

DAHI BATATA PURI

24 crisp puffed puris (as for paani puri)

1½ cups yogurt, whisked

Salt to taste

1 tablespoon sugar

2 medium potatoes, boiled and chopped

½ cup sprouted beans, blanched

1 teaspoon red chilli powder

½ teaspoon chaat masala

¼ cup Green Coriander Chutney (page 95)

¼ cup Date and Tamarind Chutney (page 94)

Sev, as required

1 teaspoon roasted cumin powder

2 tablespoons chopped fresh coriander leaves

2 tablespoons fresh pomegranate kernels

- Add salt and sugar to the yogurt and whisk till smooth. Place in a refrigerator till ready to use.

- Mix together the boiled potatoes, sprouted moong, salt, half a teaspoon of chilli powder and chaat masala.
- Make a hole in each puri, fill with the potato filling, dip in the yogurt and place on a plate.
- Alternatively, place the puris on the plate and pour the yogurt over, reserving a little for the topping.
- Place dollops of the green coriander chutney and date and tamarind chutney over the yogurt.
- Sprinkle the sev, remaining chilli powder, roasted cumin powder, coriander leaves and pomegranate over the puris, and finally top with the remaining yogurt.
- Serve immediately.

PAANI PURI

40 crisp puffed puris

1½ cups Date and Tamarind Chutney (page 94)

Filling

1 cup bean sprouts, boiled

2 large boiled potatoes cut into ¼-inch cubes

Black salt to taste

1 teaspoon chaat masala

Paani

1 small bunch (25 grams) fresh coriander leaves, chopped

1 small bunch (30 grams) fresh mint leaves, chopped

5–6 green chillies

2 tablespoons paani puri masala

½ tablespoon dried mango powder

Black salt to taste

Salt to taste

½ tablespoon roasted cumin powder

3 tablespoons lemon juice

¼ cup boondi

- To make the sprout filling, combine all the ingredients in a bowl, toss to mix well and set aside.
- To make the paani, grind the coriander leaves, mint leaves and green chillies with enough water to a paste. Transfer the ground paste to a large bowl, add the paani puri masala, dried mango powder, black salt, salt, cumin powder and lemon juice and stir to mix well.
- Stir in six cups of water and place in a refrigerator to chill. Just before serving, stir in the boondi.
- To serve, press down on the top of each puri with your thumb to make a holllow, fill with a little moong and potato filling followed by a half a tablespoon of date and tamarind chutney. Dip the puri in the prepared paani and serve immediately.

Note: For the paani, use 2–3 tablespoons of unripe green mango paste instead of lemon juice.

BISCUIT CORN SEV PURI

16 cream cracker biscuits

2 large potatoes, boiled and mashed

½ cup corn kernels, blanched

Salt to taste

¼ teaspoon red chilli powder

2 medium onions, chopped

Chaat masala, as required

8–10 teaspoons Green Coriander Chutney (page 95)

2 tablespoons Red Chilli-Garlic Chutney (page 96)

8–10 teaspoons Date and Tamarind Chutney (page 94)

1 cup fine sev

2 tablespoons chopped fresh coriander leaves

1 small unripe green mango, chopped

- Arrange four biscuits on each plate.
- In a separate bowl, mix together the mashed potatoes, corn, salt and chilli powder.

- Divide into sixteen portions. Place a portion of the potato mixture on each biscuit. Sprinkle onion and chaat masala on top.
- Drizzle half a teaspoon of green coriander chutney, one-fourth teaspoon of red chilli-garlic chutney and one teaspoon of date and tamarind chutney one over the other on each biscuit. Cover the biscuits with plenty of sev.
- Sprinkle coriander leaves and green mango on top. Serve immediately.

Chef's Tip

Add more red chilli-garlic chutney for a spicier snack.

BHEL PURI

2 cups puffed rice

1 medium onion, chopped

¼ cup roasted masala split Bengal gram

¼ cup roasted peanuts

2 medium potatoes, boiled, peeled and diced

2-3 green chillies, chopped

½ cup sev

8 crisp puris

Salt to taste

¼ cup Green Coriander Chutney (page 95)

½ cup Date and Tamarind Chutney (page 94)

2 tablespoons Red Chilli-Garlic Chutney (page 96)

1 teaspoon lemon juice

2 tablespoons chopped fresh coriander leaves

- Combine the puffed rice, onion, split masala Bengal gram, peanuts, potatoes, green chillies and half the sev in a bowl and toss well to mix.

- Add four crushed puris and salt to taste and mix again.
- Add the chutneys to taste and the lemon juice and mix well.
- Garnish with coriander leaves and the remaining sev. Serve immediately with remaining puris.

MATHRI SEV PURI

16 mathri

1 tablespoon oil

1 medium onion, chopped

1 cup American sweet corn, boiled

2 fresh red chillies, chopped

¼ cup sweet chilli sauce

½ teaspoon chaat masala

1 tablespoon chopped fresh mint leaves

2 tablespoons chopped fresh coriander leaves

Salt to taste

1 tablespoon lemon juice

½ cup sev

2 tablespoons chopped fresh parsley

- Heat the oil in a non-stick pan; add the onion and sauté till translucent.
- Add the corn and sauté for half a minute. Add the fresh red chillies, sweet chilli sauce and toss to mix.
- Add the chaat masala, mint leaves and coriander leaves and salt. Mix and cook till dry.
- Stir in the lemon juice. Divide the mixture into sixteen portions.
- Place each portion on a mathri. Sprinkle sev, garnish with parsley and serve immediately.

URAD DAL PAPAD CHAAT

10 large urad dal papads

2 teaspoons oil

¼ teaspoon mustard seeds

A pinch of asafoetida

1 large onion, chopped

1 medium cucumber, seeded and chopped

1 medium tomato, seeded and chopped

3 tablespoons chopped fresh coriander leaves

2 teaspoons chaat masala

2 teaspoons lemon juice

1 teaspoon Red Chilli-Garlic Chutney (page 96)

- Roast the papads on a non-stick tawa over a low heat pressing lightly with a piece of muslin.
- When slightly cool, crush into fine pieces with your fingers and place in a bowl and set aside.

- Heat the oil in a non-stick pan; add the mustard seeds and asafoetida. When the seeds begin to splutter, remove from heat and pour onto the crushed papads and toss well.
- Mix together the onion, cucumber, tomato, half the coriander leaves, chaat masala, lemon juice and chilli-garlic chutney and toss with the papad mixture.
- Garnish with the remaining coriander leaves and serve immediately.

DATE AND TAMARIND CHUTNEY

15–20 dates

1 cup tamarind pulp

2 teaspoons cumin seeds

¼ teaspoon fennel seeds

½ cup grated jaggery

2 teaspoons red chilli powder

1 teaspoon dried ginger powder

1 teaspoon black salt

Salt to taste

- Wash, stone dates and chop roughly. Dry-roast cumin seeds and fennel seeds. Cool slightly, and grind together to a powder.
- Mix together dates, jaggery, tamarind pulp, cumin and fennel powders, chilli powder, dried ginger powder, black salt, salt to taste and four cups of water.
- Cook over a medium heat till it comes to a boil. Lower the heat and continue to cook for six to eight minutes. Cool and serve.

GREEN CORIANDER CHUTNEY

1 cup fresh coriander leaves

½ cup fresh mint leaves

2–3 green chillies, seeded and chopped

Black salt to taste

¼ teaspoon sugar

1 teaspoon lemon juice

- Clean, wash and roughly chop coriander and mint leaves.
- In a blender, process chopped coriander and mint leaves with chopped green chillies. Make a smooth paste using a little water if required.
- Add black salt and sugar and blend again.
- Transfer to a bowl and stir in the lemon juice.

RED CHILLI-GARLIC CHUTNEY

10 dried red chillies, seeded

12 large cloves garlic, peeled and chopped

2 teaspoons lemon juice

Sea salt to taste

1 teaspoon cumin powder

- Soak red chillies in one and a half cups of water for half an hour. Drain.
- Grind the red chillies and garlic cloves with lemon juice to a fine paste.
- Add a little water if necessary.
- Add sea salt and cumin powder and mix well.